Phoe

Rises

Jason Conway

Phoenix Rises
© Jason Conway, 2019
ISBN: 9781796751857

Cover Artwork by Orion Champadiyil
Edited by Nimue Brown

Paperback first published in the UK in 2019
by Jason Conway, Gloucester

Book cover design & layout by Jason Conway
www.cre8urbrand.co.uk

Life is a blessing
so take flight
and stake your claim

Go catch that fabled dragon
for if you're fearless
all is tamed.

This book is a personal journey of transformation through the healing power of poetry, in a difficult year in my life.

The poem above captures my new outlook on life; in finding its beauty, facing my fears and following my passions, whatever they may be and wherever they may take me.

Jason Conway

A poem has the ability to place a spotlight on the soul, offering anyone who reads it a unique perspective. A poem can illuminate just as easily as it may provide comfort and reassurance during difficult times, whether due to a broken heart, or the loss of a loved one.

Sacha Hayes O'Grady - Torquay, Victoria, Australia
https://themoonunderwater.org

In this book I have complied a collection of thirteen dark poems and thirteen light poems to illustrate how my writing swayed from sadness to great joy during a difficult time.

The light poems are a celebration of the best of life and the great beauty of the natural world. I often refer to Mother in my writing. Mother being Mother Earth or Mother Nature, the guiding force in creation and the great renewer of life. I have a very strong connection to nature and draw energy from it. It influences pretty much everything I do and shapes my dreams and hopes for life.

Nature, art and poetry are my solace, my muse and my sage and they help to steer me through difficult periods. Poetry especially, has the capacity to channel my thoughts and gift me the tools to express myself openly and honestly.

I use the word 'possession' to describe my relationship with my poetry intentionally, as inspiration frequently takes hold of me and compels me to write. Once finished, I read back my work the next day with confusion and amazement, as I'm often unable to remember writing parts of, or even entire poems. Something inside takes over and wills me to write.

Elizabeth Gilbert in her wonderful book 'Big Magic' talks about ideas as though they are entities, spirits that find willing hosts to birth them into reality. I love this notion that we are not directly inspired to create great beauty, but are influenced by floating entities to truly express our latent creativity. But the caveat to this is that we have to be receptive and willing to accept them and bring them to life. Looking back at my work and my blank memories of writing, would certainly support this notion. Whatever you believe, something guides me to write and helps me to heal myself and grow with words.

I practice mindfulness in nature which goes hand in hand with the healing force that has been guiding me through my years of change. Poetry has been a great calling for me and for that I am truly humbled by and thankful for.

I hope you enjoy these poems and perhaps are inspired to start writing, take up art, begin a new creative hobby, or try something new. At the very least, I hope you seek your own escapes into nature to be inspired by Mother, Gaia (or whatever guiding force you believe in) and all her gifts.

We all go through dark times in our life, but life finds a way of shining hope on us and finding inspiration and joy within. We just have to be open to change when it finds us.

Little did I know at the time, but during a family holiday in Woolacombe in July 2016, I would start my journey into poetry.

During a surfing lesson I discovered something deeply personal and transformative. I have always had an affinity with the sea, which is expected for a water sign such as the crab, and to use an animal metaphor, I took to it like a duck to water. Being able to stand on a foam board on top of a wave was incredible, to say the least, and it gave me a great sense of being at one with the power of the sea, a master of my own course.

I can still vividly remember floating in the sea, draped over the board and gazing out toward the horizon, when something changed. My epiphany flooded my brain with thoughts of life, purpose and wonder. In a split second the sea was calm, the wind froze and the water felt like air, with me suspended in thought. Soon after the lesson was over and everything felt bright, hyper-real and I wore a wide smile for the rest of the day.

Something was pulling me back to the static caravan, something giving me the compulsion to write a poem. I can't explain what or why, but I knew that I just needed to write. Back at the caravan I got out my pad and a pen and within about 30 minutes I was finished. During the writing I was filled with flashbacks and daydreams of myself as a passenger in the ocean and a passenger through life. That poem is called Life's Water Dance.

My sea of calm, power and infinite grace,
I hear your call oh wondrous place.

Waves of elemental energy cleanse the soul,
away from chatter, crowd and road.

Air's fresh saline scent carried o'er breeze,
unlocking maps of sense and memory.

Adrift the tides of life, bound by moon and sun,
calm of mind and perspective anew.

Visions of brave new worlds beyond horizons wall,
grand journeys steered by Neptune's call.

Fleeting glimpses of passengers' rock and shell,
each with majestic tales to tell.

Of distant shores and long lost hosts,
coming to rest on the grained carpet of ancestors.

Enriched with sense of place in oceans vast expanse,
to pause and savour life's water dance.

Back in October 2016, I received a Facebook message from a friend who used to teach me martial arts. He asked if I would be interested in joining his new poetry group, The Gloucester Poetry Society, that he was starting up. I'd only ever written one serious poem and that was back in July, but I didn't hesitate to join.

By January 2017 I had caught the passion for poetry and was already willing to help promote the Society and help to organise a new open mic event in Gloucester. This quickly became a monthly event and I was trying out reading my poetry in public. Daunting at first, but over a relatively short space of time I grew in confidence to feel comfortable performing my work in front of people. This was one of my challenges to better myself.

I quickly became obsessed by poetry and had become a prolific writer. I simply love to write and try to express my thoughts in this new medium. I loved the challenges of trying out different forms of poetry and trying to take myself out of the world around me to look at it differently and interpret it in new ways.

Fast forward to October 2017 and I had successfully crowdfunded a poetry anthology for the Society and was helping to organise our first Poetry Festival to celebrate the Society's first anniversary, not to mention hosting several open mic events locally. I had also become a published poet, something I had never dreamed would happen, back when I was floating in the sea in Woolacombe.

This was all a fantastic rollercoaster of new experiences and one that I simply loved being part of. Poetry had become part of my life, part of me. I had found a whole new friend circle of poets from across the country and across the globe.

I'd like to have said that this was all planned out, but the truth is that it wasn't. This all came about from a chance email from a friend and by me saying yes to a new opportunity and sticking with it. Through the beautiful chaos of my poetic journey, great things happened for me. But, the best part of it was witnessing the transformation of a small group of poets sharing their work, to a nationally known poetry society that is making waves, with poets from around the world sharing their work in an all inclusive community.

I have met some truly inspirational people through poetry and The Gloucester Poetry Society, some that I am honoured to call my friends. Some have gone through great troubles and personal battles and came out the other side, through the healing power of poetry, and that is a great blessing that I have experienced too.

Call it fate or call it chance, but poetry had changed my life for the better. It gifted me a new love and a new talent, a new creative outlet that was rich in life, visceral in reflection and contemplation, and inspirational and empowering in the extreme.

Poetry opened something within me, a new creative renaissance if you will, one that greatly benefited my art, my design, my outlook on life and had given me a new found confidence and a hope for the future.

Contents

WORDS

OF

DARK

TO

LIGHT

Lost at sea my sail hangs still
comfort yearned beyond reflection's eye
I free a thought, let it fly to a new home
will its feathers bend to keeper's quill?

Alone I drift cracked lipped and sombre
muted by introversion's glare
solitude's prison keeps the soul chilled
thoughts of 'we' petrified on singular tundra.

Once consoled by the harbour of companion
the stillness of 'I' has no wind nor sail
now all but 'me' is starved by salt
adrift the endless sea of abandon.

Plans seem hollow somehow
my journey shrouded in 'lone' mists
no sign ahead nor welcome cry
just empty triumphs locked below.

Contemplation's optimist sparks a new trail
and warms the shy hull of my boat
'tis feathered note kept corked in bottle
a breeze of hope to fill my sail.

Gathered pace held fast for ground
of cryptic place in sender's map
silhouetted figure spied on distant rock
new friend found to treat my wound.

Mother's Gift

Azure splendour of rapturous light
evaporate the veil of charcoal slumber
creature and plant bathed in bright
bask in Mother's gifted wonder.

Breathe sweet elixir and ponder
casuality's journey hath begun
catch the tail of time and ride yonder
to chase day's sighted freedom.

Fate's web to some already spun.
Flee apathy's roots binding fear
to embrace curiosity's fiery sun
and live tales for young to hear.

The winds of life are joy to steer
a journey of Did instead of Might
your life will sing in stories dear
as you pass through soil to light.

A creep of doom rakes the neck
chilled cones sparked to attention
saline dew breaks resting skin
primal fear takes hold again
wrenched from sleep and calm is gone
to visioned loss, drawn in fated deck.

Oblivion flashes in the sable abyss
what's next after death
if there is a next?
which god to strike a pact
or sentient force to submit beneath
to ensure kaleidoscopic bliss?

Heartbroken kin left in sorrow
to carve out their smited path
the forced crown of elders
will bestow a raft of deciding doors
set by deity or random math
or lit by Mother's loving glow?

Rapid gasps fuel a panicked heart
throat burns with acid flares
body locked taut and frozen
time to be cast out or chosen
consumed by fire or free from tears
or gifted rebirth for second start?

Trials of life drop anchor
and dredge the pit of hopelessness
to stir the mind with horror
metalled taste spikes oily and raw
in tongues muted confession
as voice thrashes behind locked jaws.

Silent notes without a bark
eyelids peeled by invisible threads
creaks and shadows, lungs fall dense
A shaded watcher casts their presence
ice prickled sweat filled with dread
'tis clock's last tick struck in this bed.

Seeds of Dreams

The seeds of dreams await the breeze
to sail above with hope to seize.

Soon to root and plant that hope
and keep all of our dreams afloat.

Myths to some perceived as weeds
so look within for truth to heed.

This tufted lion in the rough
renewed by air to call fear's bluff.

Singeing pain burns the veins
like acid strips the paint from steel.
Being lost can challenge the quo,
but having lost is the truest dread.

This rouge elixir drains from frame
till cold and numb remains.
Incinerated glee lost in sorrow's vortex,
ripping the soul from these bones.

An after-shocked silence quakes balance
and scrambles every fleeting thought,
as lava scalds this naked shredded throat,
turning fleeing words to ash.

Boiling needles of steam blind the eyes
and sweated skin frozen to touch,
by a venomous and suffocating ill wind
with devilled fingers to wrap and choke.

This world lies cracked and scarred
like a flawed diamond bleeding light,
all that has gone is gone for good
replaced by creeping, crushing doubt.

For what now follows is bleak,
filled with an inky cloud of loss and fear.
Once wrapped tight with joy and hope
my drained shell can no longer find a tear.

Rivers of salty agony
have left a sore and blistered mask.
This fractured man sees the future
as an insurmountable task.

Freed to Dream

Dynamic spiral blooms to life
A coded destiny bound in charge
Sparked in the invisible domain.

Gathering pace towards ethereal light
Thoughts to sounds, to screams of rage
Escape to air and world of pain.

Flourished growth in mind and height
Endless wonder by organic mage
Born to world of cosmic grains.

Descend to end as soul takes flight
Essence sheds the mortal cage
Freed to dream through spatial plane.

Dynamic spiral blooms to life
Descend to end as soul takes flight.

I once soared with joy
Till wings of denial burned
Left raw and bleeding
Stranded soul in cold new world
The mask of content left scars.

Uneasy signals
Kept at bay in fear of quake
To end my safe world
Up manned, cruel music faced
To join a sea of lonely stars.

My dependency
Blinded truth's reality
We're better apart
To be the best we can be
In pursuit of love so pure.

Altered States

For every beginning, there is an end
a before to every after
each open draws a close
like a thought becomes a legend.

We are all born to a start
our sails race to journey's anchor
all ends hail in the new
voids filled when we depart.

Our memory begins with fondness
in the minds of those we cherish
family and friends held dear
those we bathed in kindness.

Empty shells to fill the soil
our warmth to spawn creation
birthing creature and plant
'til our bones echo the past.

Energy shifts to altered states
ripples in a random sea.
The cosmic blacksmith's hinge
swings choice to fortune's gate.

The pessimist spies a fearful end
with change, the welcome optimist
push meets pull on life's scales
equal and opposite in mirrored bond.

Do we join a single force
or see cascades of rebirth?
Will we join those who left
or can we master our own course?

Sometimes best is not good enough to justify the means, even if no alternative can be found.

Sometimes the burden of doubt seeps through the skin in a teared descent to the ground.

Sometimes pain is not felt at all, but nonetheless, envelopes a loving soul in numbness.

Sometimes apathy washes away the blanket of hope, leaving me exposed, just an empty withered mess.

Sometimes silent words are wept without will or anticipation, from twin deserts burned so they cannot see.

Sometimes bleakness and isolation bring respite to the broken soul devoid of joy, still raw within me.

Sometimes the community of company is the least we need, to feed our hungry hearts.

Sometimes sustenance has no place for revival, to feed a black hole, consumed by galaxies of shattered smiles.

Sometimes time slows to an ebb and a vast expanse of introspection weighs heavily on my bones.

Sometimes the cold is a welcome guest, to chill the seething acid fire scorching weary lungs.

For tomorrow is but a faded dream where my pain can be absolved.

Love, Learn, Dream, Repeat

Love, learn, dream, repeat
go build a world for hope to keep
think bold and bright in wonder stare
wear hearted sleeves soul fruit to bear
treat all with warmth as friend not foe
steer joy to where your journey goes
smile eyes with kind to spread your light
and fly your dreams on possible kites
live this motto and hold it deep
Love, learn, dream, repeat.

I've had a bad day
but it's nothing major
just enough to tip my scales
and flare up all those daily fails
I know what I need to feel fine
I'll grab myself a glass of wine.

Yes, that's so much better
as my stress is receding
turning the bad to funny tales
a snigger builds to bellowing whales
I know what I need to pass the time
I'll grab myself a glass of wine.

Hang on, what's that lurking
in the bowels of my mind
something malign to brew up a gale
agitation turns to anger on my bed of nails
up early, who cares, I'll be fine
this king of rage needs another wine.

Power pulsing through my veins
I set the world to rights
intoxicated and heading for the rails
a heavy heart with aches and ails
fists clenched and teeth in grind
where's that damn bottle of wine.

Clouds fog inside my head
and they quickly mist my eyes
leaded eyelids on magnetic pales
bravado deflated by drunken sails
I'll embrace the numbness, it's limbo time
bottle's empty, no more wine.

Welcome to the morning thunder
a day of pain ahead
I thought I was fine, but life's derailed
haunted by loss and a love that failed
another night wasted, seduced by wine
I just need a friend to share some time.

Travelling Without Moving

I sit here perplexed by a notion of change
with no recollection of where I've been
or indeed, where I'm supposed to be.
For I am caught in a spectacular daydream
where endless possibilities roam with glee
and infinite journeys are made by playful eyes.

This is my now, my real and my heart is free,
for I am the god of this shift shaping destiny.

The realm of yes with chains unshackled
and ties that bind conformity's bruises,
no control by others with interests vested
or the empty chilled boredom of mundanity.
All can be done with a single thought
by matter recompiled into boundless desires.

This is my now, my real and my heart is free,
for I am the god of this shift shaping destiny.

I can build empires to rule with loving hands
or birth planets from dancing cranial sparks,
carve galaxies with fingers in cosmic dust
and pirouette multiverses as they fractal into life.
All existence is formed from a whim or a will,
the traps of time now freely put to bed.

This is my now, my real and my heart is free,
for I am the god of this shift shaping destiny.

Reality laws, popped like soaped bubbles
in vast reaching oceans of my limitless mind,
floating towards chaotic maelstrom skies
like free radical spies cast out of a dream.
Impossible thoughts embraced into life
waving bye to rules, cast fleetingly aside.

This is my now, my real and my heart is free,
for I am the god of this shift shaping destiny.

My time here is governed only by doubt
of what could happen if two of us were about.
Someone to share with, to laugh and to love
and challenge our fears with gifts of abundance.
Set sail to new shores where joy is the breeze
that tickles our lungs with scented smiles.

This is my now, my real and my heart is free,
for I am the god of this shift shaping destiny.

So, the notion of change that grew at the start,
fermented a while till times cork came unstuck.
I now sit in a park, by a face so hypnotic
that I stare in awe, struck by her warmth.
We smile and engage in a sweet river of discourse,
fluttering signals magnified by Cupid's fated darts.

This is my now, my real and my heart's given free,
For life's now our daydream made real by thee.

Departing teardrops
Family separated
Shared magnetic bonds.

Learn in retrospect
Unchartered worlds to conquer
Many longing thoughts.

Travelling thoughts fly
Wanderlust to constant flux
Inquisitive life
Fear sinks comfort's roots to core
Hope's silken wings let you soar

Dream with open eyes
Turn every corner and bend
Pursue unknown truth
Drink the ocean of culture
And live a journey so pure.

I am alone
a lone soul
with a hole to fill
in a void that's still
like a well in a desert
stranded in an arid expanse
or a shout under water
muffled by the current's stir
for my bed is cursed
half a frozen lake
half barely warm
haunted by the ghosts of joy
long faded, wintered and forlorn
paled by the reflection of ancient times
and like a proud lion scarred by thorns
I scratch my tired sides at first dawn
tearing deep to the blood burning inside
once warmly flooded with passion's tide.

Volcanic heat now all but turned to stone
as the echo of compassion
spans a boned chasm
like a dove without a shore
a bird without its call
a tongue without a throat
a cargo with no boat
a fingerless hand
a grain of sand devoid of coast

a lens without its scope.
I sift through powdered memories
so frail they feel but a dream
someone else's preordained scheme
but respite is eagerly found
in the distraction of company
of family, friends and the joy of others
benefactors of empathy
as my heart rests, empty paper thin
longing for the crackle of dark magic
to cast its mythical prediction
and heal this Olympian tragedy.

Let the great gods of old
sew back the tear in this icy sky
and bring the stars back aligned
flee sirens of doubt from this misted mind
with Zeus's scorn filled gales
electrified thunderclaps to bolster my sails
and send a shockwave
through the corpse of emptiness
that numbing tar eyed temptress.

Draw her back to the lair of Hades
to claw no more at my gravelled knees
and release imprisoned regret
so I can once more straighten my gait
and spy beyond the blackened silhouette
of a sombre puppet show
heckled by the cackling shadows

of my saddened legend.
May I stare at the charred heavens
as I leave the calm of this hurricane's eye
and let it rip the flesh of my sorrow
clean from these weighted ribs
let those angry winds shatter my sighs
and bring forth a blanket of healing skies
to wrap my future in hopeful skin
fill my lungs with expansive optimism
melt the lead in my heels
and mend the grain leaked holes
of my time-locked hourglass
so that its shifting sands
can draw change near
and grant these three wishes
to learn how to be
to lift the veil and see
and for I to be we.

I Blame Books

In business, why are we taught
to practice busyness?

Surely work should be a pleasure
not rushed or stressed
make it slower, more relaxed
we'd all be so much happier
if we just busied less.

For me, less is more, I always say
think smart, work smart
and make more time for healthy hearts.

So I read books to better myself
think differently, expand my mind
teaching me to leave the daily bind.

I took time out and learnt new skills
to enjoy a life of ventured thrills
now I work when and where I like
with people of passion and minds alike.

My work is now my play
with so much fun to do each day
and in so many ways.
How's that I hear you say?
Well, I help people to love their space
and fill it with joyous grace.

So read a book, I dare you to
and your life might just change
as help is there on the page
in books that show you how to flee your cage
to swap the nine to five and take your chance
for a life of adventure and abundance.

Yes, go pinch yourself, it's very real
go swap the old for passions real
mix things up and break the norm
be a shining light from the raging storm
and build a life full of feel
to ditch the chains for smile appeal.

No-one was hurt in this unbelievable tale
I just learned how to blow my sails
and embark upon a thrilling journey
with a mind rewired for a better way.
so, if you're curious and would like to see
go follow my lead for lifestyle glee!

The house of unspeakable dwells inside
scratching the fleshy surface of sanity
a penned beckoning stokes its rage

Pale guise of horror ensnares the kind
chilled by the creep of hellish destiny
knotted beneath its blackened pages

Quilled drug of fear does here reside
rocking all noble, humble and gentry
narcotic screams rattle cranial cage

Vanquished hopes of light have died
all haste, scribed death of chastity
this fated tome bound by onyx sage

Cimmerian beasts gnaw on human rind
adrenal tempests tip scales of parity
abominable dread unleashed by inky mage

Nightmarish havoc is enshrined
this fibred thread of hellish morality
bound in fright to scare through ages.

The Silent Quest

Shut the door to your soul, let it sleep a while
inside it will dream of wonders fantastic
love to clear doubt under shimmering skies
elation to warm your fluttering lungs
not a sound outside, just contented breath
calm in the joy of your silent quest
evoke the true seeker from your visioned pause
and follow your heart that shines with new cause.

I keep my pets hungry
trapped in my mind
a cage left unrattled
my monsters are fine
they growl at my pain
like acid
stripping atrophy
bones clean
raw from the fray
daily doubt
gnaws at my gates
rusting with each attack
torrents of insecurity
relentless
unhindered
narcotic

For I am consumed
by fire and stone brimmed
rivers of lava
devour all that's good
leaving red and black
from the beasts attack
evil and sorrow
fear and sleep
shadows to reap

I am broken
cracked

blacked
a fading token
of self
as blood runs open
wounds unspoken
hidden from view
and kept locked
in Jones' locker
under crushing seas
of unease

The black sister teases
a shouldered muse
whispering wired barbs
that rip without mercy
heresy
to believe I was free
from the other me
the one that cowers
dreamless
cold
and hollow

Dark rages
blind fury's
thrashing
indiscriminate
peeling away pages
leathered words
burned with hot irons

under tarnished skin
unforgiven

An oilless man of tin
seized
bled
empty of hope
an unlit candle
lost
security tossed
aside
left to fester
as the rot spreads

Time is still
brain lies ill
poisoned by pills
of bitterness
regrets
joy to forget
walls crumble
tombs unearthed
quaking
taking
my will
like a wolf to a flock
thoughts amok
racing for weakness
searching for unturned proof
riddles unwritten

by the gods
stricken
in my glass prison
a birdless cage
with nowhere to hide

Bleak futures spied
hope to deride
before I wake
to gaze at future's mirror
to seek but a smile
a grain of empathy
as the grass of envy
blankets
the fortunes of others
for love is theirs
hope in pairs

Dry tears
ghost empty ducts
dust settled
on opportunity
like a keyless lock
shackled
restrained
subservient
to a spiralling master
dreams to shatter
shards to pitter
and patter

like fallen stars
wept from the heavens

I keep my pets hungry
till my new face is found.

Snak3sk1ns

Unhappy with me
I set a thought in motion
Butterfly effect
Oh, fluttering seeds of change
Please take root and set me free

Do ideas live?
Seeking out hosts to transform
Gifted transcendence
Attuned to the universe
Subconscious causality

Truth, beauty and love
Proudly worn on honest sleeves
Utopian dreams
Radiating compassion
Rippling light o'er timeless sea

I welcome in change
And learn truth in constancy
Serendipity
The snakeskins of self, shed
To invoke ascendency.

Shipwrecked

Baneful claws infect
Ending restful sleep for sweat
Augmented horrors
Scratching slumbered hope-filled doors
Terrified dreams sink shipwrecked

Wonderment frozen
Ailing heart trembling, laid bare
Lone crew abandoned
Killed by salted beasts of doom
Silenced soul mourned by full moon

Nighted steeds trample
Innocent dreams left unborn
Gales whip a beached hull
Howling banshee of remorse
Tugs my windless sails apart

Moored in raw tempest
Alone in naked despair
Revenant awakes
Elysium fields burning
Sleep bequeathed to raging sea

Terrified dreams sink shipwrecked
Sleep bequeathed to raging sea
fearful tears bloodstain the decks
haunted by the ghosts of me.

The Colours of Creation

Our world blooms into birth
from the richness of earth
to the dewy composition of clouds
and vast waters that team with creation.
Streams and rivers spread tentacles
tickling the soil to make us smile
a magical mix that sparks life
to astound the stars with its beauty.
From seeds shoot flora of infinitesimal type
coating the ground in the colours of life
and hugging the grained floor
like a silken duvet at night.
Microscopic cells join and multiply
an invisible potion stirred by Mother
the greatest magician of all
she sends us gifts so plentiful
so wonderful
so powerful
so graceful.
For that we are truly in her debt
blessed with senses six
each piece jigsawed together
to form our sense of place.
Her colours bathe us in respect
like sunlight milk to nourish our souls
and blankets of wildflowers to roll in
to rekindle the happiness of the child in us all.
Four seasons shift gracefully

in the eternal wheel of life and death
nothing is wasted and all is reclaimed
children of Mother to replenish another.
The multitude of colour delights our eyes
close them often and smell her joy
let it gift you a private screening
of memories kept safe in your mind.
Let scents become colour and shape and life
breathe deep and exhale
let your daydreams take flight
and fill your lungs with sweet history.
Take joy that your sighs feed flower, bush and tree
that keep earth alive so effortlessly
they feast upon your carbon breeze
to perpetuate our living dreams.
Symbiotic bonds of animal, creature and plant
play together on the scales of life
a seesaw ride in perfect balance
with love and hope at every glance.
Thank you, Mother, for painting
our picture in a rainbow of life
that shines from your treasured pearl
across an endless celestial sea.
Awash with splendour your heartfelt blend
is for us to embrace and softly tend
before we drift to a changed state
and in thanks renourish your land.

I bleed at night
stinging wires barb at flesh
jarring dreams as frost splinters
crystal shards cage hope in glass
a million needles bind winter's shawl
woven taught with iron angst
as armour turns to coffin
in a long forgotten grave
my flowerless cage

I bleed at night
a bloated pincushion for a heart
each prick filled with storm
each beat charged by lightning screams
to boil poisoned tar filled vats
that scar the last guards
of a long-ruined kingdom
with a crestless tattered sail
lashed by lava filled hail

I heal in light
when the black steads depart
swollen rivers of fire crust
as sleep flashes to warming haze
soothing shallow pools of tears
evaporating acid sweats
with silken sun drenched hope
a new day to fight the good fight
and banish the pain for light

I heal in light
night scars burnt from inside
have much time to heal
each friendly face to glow
and happy thoughts to seed
I need an oak to bind the ground
to bring new fruits to bear
soak my soul in amber rays
with dreams that weave my days.

If You're Fearless All Is Tamed

Go dream
with all your might
rock the very fabric
of existence.

Let aspirations
charge the universe
with a shimmering sun
of abundance.

Be contagious
with radiant positivity
bathe in the certainty
of self-belief.

Banish vampires
that drain pure joy
back to shaded pits
of woe, beneath.

For anything
will be possible
if you freely believe
in yourself.

Knowledge will
unlock your potential
so immerse your hope
in the ink of wealth.

Free dive
head first and eyes wide
into lucid pools
of endless possibility.

Magnetise
your soulful mind
with adaption
and agility.

Shine brightly
and let the mystical
wings of change
flock to your flame.

Embrace
new challenges
as just by trying
everything is gained.

Gift gravity
to spirited notions
in search of
primed hosts.

Set sail
for the truth
and ride your journey
to bountiful coasts.

For life
is a blessing
so take flight
and stake your claim.

Go catch
that fabled dragon
for if you're fearless
all is tamed.

The Oyster Bears Fruit

I'm treading water
With chains of doubt tugging heels
Suffocated dreams

Intense gravity
My foetal tears bleed at night
A seed waits for breeze

Invisible me
Painful superpower shields
Cut marionette

Lost in empty smiles
A yolk weeps in broken shell
The thorned keep in myth

The Sleeper rises
Love unravels bandages
Butterfly at dawn

A history healed
The world bathed in sunlit hope
Ink dries on new page

An oyster bears fruit
The treasure of friends and kin
Cornucopia.

Love is the Answer

There will always be people
that we meet through life
who will cause us pain
through intent or reaction
but it's who you choose to be with
that can heal you with love

There will always be people
that we meet through life
who will bring us joy
through intent or reaction
but it's who you choose to stay with
that can shield you with their love

There will always be people
that we meet through life
who will stir up anger
through intent or reaction
but it's how you choose to face it
that can hurt or show your love

There will always be people
that we meet through life
who will bring us hope
through intent or reaction
but if you choose to share it
you can fill the world with love

Will you heal
or will you shield
will you show
or will you share
love is the answer
so, shine it everywhere.

About Jason Conway

Born in Staffordshire and currently living in Gloucestershire, Jason Conway is a published poet with a true passion for nature. He is a member of The Gloucester Poetry Society and regularly attends open mic events. His poetry journey started in July 2016 after experiencing an epiphany whilst surfing, where he was compelled to write and he hasn't looked back since. He uses the pen name of The Ink Warrior.

Jason's biggest inspiration for his work is the beauty of the natural world. He is passionate about the environment and humanity's progressive devastation of it and strives to educate people to reconnect with nature. Jason is also an artist, designer and photographer, always studying his surroundings for ideas and connections.

www.facebook.com/jasonconwaypoetry
www.inkwarriorpoetry.co.uk

Beauty surrounds us
so often
overlooked

Understated
unrealised

Round the corner
underfoot
or to the skies

All I did
was open my eyes

Printed in Great Britain
by Amazon